The Brothers Size

A part of the Brother/Sister Plays

Tarell Alvin McCraney

The UK premiere of *The Brothers Size* was
a co-production between the Young Vic and ATC and opened
at the Drum Theatre Plymouth on 10 October 2007.

It was revived as a co-production between the Young Vic
and ATC at the Young Vic on 19 January 2018.

Oshoosi	**Jonathan Ajayi**
Ogun	**Sope Dirisu**
Elegba	**Anthony Welsh**
Live Sound	**Manuel Pinheiro**
Direction	**Bijan Sheibani**
Design	**Patrick Burnier**
Light	**Mike Gunning**
Sound	**Manuel Pinheiro**
Movement	**Aline David**
Vocal Musical Director	**Michael Henry**
Casting	**Amy Ball CDG**
Voice & Dialect	**Michaela Kennan**
Trainee Assistant Directors	**Tristan Fynn-Aiduenu**
	Leian John-Baptiste
Stage Manager	**Sarah Stott**
Deputy Stage Manager	**Natalie Braid**
Costume Supervisor	**Bryony Fayers**
Lighting Operator	**Nick Di Gravio/Alecs Maclennan**
Duty Sound Technician	**Aiwan Obinyan**

Tristan Fynn-Aiduenu and Leian John-Baptiste
are supported through the Boris Karloff Trainee
Assistant Directors Program at the Young Vic.

We would like to thank
Beataboutthebush, Stage Sound Services,
Unison Colour and St Mary Abbots Centre.

The Young Vic 2018 season is generously supported by
Garfield Weston Foundation, Genesis Foundation,
The Richenthal Foundation, The Sackler Trust
and an anonymous donor.

JONATHAN AJAYI | Oshoosi

Theatre includes: *A Midsummer Night's Dream in New Orleans* (Arts Theatre), *Sucker Punch, Port, Duchess of Malfi, A New Brain, The Lady from the Sea* (LAMDA).

Film includes: *Hallelujah.*

SOPE DIRISU | Ogun

Theatre includes: *Coriolanus, Pericles* (RSC); *One Night in Miami* (Donmar); *The Whipping Man* (Theatre Royal Plymouth); *Tory Boyz, Romeo and Juliet, Prince of Denmark* (in West End) and *Our Days Of Rage* (all National Youth Theatre).

Television includes: *Guiding Light, Five by Five, The Halcyon, Black Mirror, Undercover, Siblings, Humans, The Casual Vacancy, The Mill* and *Utopia.*

Film includes: *Sand Castle, The Huntsman* and *Criminal.*

ANTHONY WELSH | Elegba

Young Vic includes: *The Brothers Size, dirty butterfly, Blackta.*

Theatre includes: *Barber Shop Chronicles, Nut* (National Theatre); *The Merchant of Venice* (Almeida); *Precious Little Talent, E–Z, Lower Ninth* (Trafalgar Studios); *Sucker Punch* (Royal Court); *Pornography* (Tricycle Theatre and tour).

Television includes: *Black Mirror: Crocodile, Fleabag. The Secrets, Life's Too Short* and *Top Boy.*

Film includes: *The Arrival, Ibiza, Journeyman, Sand Castle, The Girl with All the Gifts, Second Coming, Starred Up, Dirty Money, My Brother the Devil* and *Comes a Bright Day.*

TARELL ALVIN McCRANEY

Tarell is best known for the Oscar-winning film *Moonlight (*Best Film and Best Adapted Screenplay), which was based on his script *In Moonlight Black Boys Look Blue*. For theatre, his trilogy *The Brother/Sister Plays*, which consists of *The Brothers Size*, *In The Red and Brown Water* and *Marcus or the Secret of Sweet*, has been widely performed. Other plays include his edit of *Antony and Cleopatra* (RSC, Public Theater NY and Gable Stage Miami), *Head of Passes* (Steppenwolf Theater, Berkeley Rep, Public Theater), *Choir Boy* (Royal Court, Manhattan Theater Club), *Without/Sin* and *Run, Mourner and Run, The Breach* and *Wig Out!* (Vineyard Theater, Royal Court). Tarell is the recipient of a MacArthur 'Genius' Grant, the Whiting Award, Steinberg Playwright Award, the Evening Standard Most Promising Playwright Award, the New York Times Outstanding Playwright Award, the Paula Vogel Playwriting Award, the Windham Campbell Award, and a Doris Duke Artist Award. Tarell is the Chair of the Playwriting Department at Yale School of Drama.

BIJAN SHEIBANI | Direction

Bijan Sheibani's first production at the Young Vic was *The Brothers Size* in 2007, revived in 2008 and co-produced with ATC, where Bijan was Artistic Director 2007–2010. He also directed *Eurydice* by Sarah Ruhl at the Young Vic in 2010, co-produced with ATC and Drum Theatre Plymouth. Most recently he directed Inua Ellams' new play *Barber Shop Chronicles* at the National Theatre, produced by Fuel, the National Theatre and West Yorkshire Playhouse. His recent production of *Nothing* for Glyndebourne was nominated for a 2017 Southbank Sky Arts Award for Best Opera. He was an Associate Director of the National Theatre from 2010–2015. Theatre credits at the National Theatre include: *Our Class* (Olivier nomination for Best Director), *The Kitchen*, *A Taste of Honey*, *Emil and the Detectives* and *Romeo and Juliet*. Other theatre credits include *Giving* (Hampstead), *The House of Bernarda Alba* (Almeida), *Moonlight* (Donmar), *The Typist* (ATC/Riverside/Sky Arts), *Ghosts* (ATC/Arcola), *Other Hands* and *Flush* (Soho Theatre) *and Gone Too Far!* (Royal Court/Hackney Empire/Albany/ATC) which won an Olivier award in 2009 for Outstanding Achievement in an Affiliate Theatre. Film credits include *Groove is in the Heart*, which was selected for the BFI London Film Festival 2014 and *Samira's Party*, produced by Film London and the BFI as part of the 2017 London Calling Plus scheme, and also selected for the BFI London Film Festival 2017.

Bijan's opera credits include *Nothing* (Glyndebourne / Danish National Opera), *The Virtues of Things* and *Through His Teeth* (Royal Opera House) and *Tarantula in Petrol Blue* (Aldeburgh). Future engagements include the Australian tour of *Barber Shop Chronicles*, a new production of *Circle Mirror Transformation* by Annie Baker for Home Manchester, and *Tell Me the Truth about Love*, a new opera for Streetwise Opera.

PATRICK BURNIER | Design

Young Vic includes: *The Brothers Size* (with ATC), *After Miss Julie, Joe Turner's Come and Gone, Eurydice* (with ATC).

Other theatre includes: *Il Va Vous Arriver Quelque Chose, Dr Incubis / Impact* (Théâtre 2·21, Switzerland); *Enquette Magnetique* (Festival de la Cité, Lausanne); *Pinocchio* (Le Petit Theatre); *A Christmas Carol, Small Change* (Sherman Cymru); *A Miracle* (Royal Court); *Living the Eucharist, The Wemmick Story* (UK tour); *Le Petit Tailleur* (Moulin-Neuf Theatre); *Gaudeamus, Night Just Before the Forests* (Arcola Theatre) and *In The Jungle of the Cities* (RADA).

Dance includes: *Entity* (Sadler's Wells, nominated for a 2009 South Bank Show Award) and *Shore* (site-specific).

MIKE GUNNING | Light

Young Vic includes: *The Brothers Size* (also UK tour); *The Emperor, Kafka's Monkey* (both also HOME Manchester, Theatre Royal Winchester); *Eurydice* (with ATC) and *Measure for Measure* (RSC).

Other theatre includes: *Uncle Vanya, Inkheart, The Fun Fair, Romeo and Juliet* (HOME Manchester), *I Capture the Castle* (Watford Palace Theatre); *King Lear* (Old Vic, as Associate Lighting Designer); *Crime And Punishment* (Moscow Musical Theatre); *Rime of the Ancient Mariner* (BAM); *The Drowned Man* (site-specific for Punchdrunk/National Theatre); *The Snow Queen* (Rose Theatre Kingston); *The Resistible Rise of Arturo Ui* (Liverpool Everyman).

Opera includes: *The Magic Flute, The Marriage of Figaro, Pirates of Penzance, Ernani, Il Trovatore* (ENO); *Macbeth, Albert Herring, Lucio Silla, Y Tŵr* (Buxton Festival); *La Traviata* (Wiener Festwochen); *Dido and Aeneas* (Théâtre National de l'Opéra-comique); *Eugene Onegin, Don Giovanni* (British Youth Opera, Peacock Theatre); *Manon Lescaut, Fedora* (Holland Park Opera).

MANUEL PINHEIRO | Sound

Young Vic includes: *The Brothers Size*, *Eurydice*, *Play Size*, *Paper Promises*.

Other theatre includes: *A Song Inside* (Gate Theatre), *A Woman Alone* (Tabard Theatre); *Doris Day Can F**k Off* (Camden People's Theatre); *So Just Stories* (STK); *The Jewish Wife* (Battersea Arts Centre).

Dance credits: *The Adaption Contraption* (Regionteatern Blekinge Kronoberg, Sweden); *The Door* (South East Dance); *Not What I Had in Mind* (The Place, Swindon Dance, Fringe Festival, Danseteliers Rotterdam, CNDB Bucharest); *Red T-Shirt Project* (Evoé, Lisbon, Portugal); *The Thing* (The Place, Dance4, South East Dance), *THINGINESS, THINGUMMY, THINGUMAJIG & THINGIWHATSIT* (Sadler's Wells, The Place) *He Alone Who Gains the Youth, Gains the Future* (The Place); *Live, with the certain tendencies of robin dingemans & mihaela dancs* (The Place).

ALINE DAVID | Movement

Young Vic includes: *Dutchman*, *Elektra*, *The Invisible Woman*, *The Brothers Size*, *Play Size*.

Other theatre includes: *The Barbershop Chronicles*, *The Kitchen*, *Romeo and Juliet*, *A Taste of Honey*, *Emil and The Detectives*, *Antigone* (National Theatre); *Macbeth*, *The Merchant of Venice* (RSC); *Nothing* (Glyndebourne), *The Tempest* (Theatre Northhampton); *The Mighty Walzer* (Royal Exchange); *The Iphigenia Quartet* (Gate Theatre); *First Love is the Revolution* (Soho Theatre); *Romeo and Juliet* (Sheffield Crucible); *Much Ado About Nothing, All the Angels: Handel and the First Messiah* (Globe); *Proof* (Menier Chocolate Factory); *The House of Bernarda Alba* (Almeida Theatre); *Gone Too Far!* (Royal Court/UK tour, winner of 2008 Olivier Award for Outstanding Achievement in an Affiliate Theatre).

MICHAEL HENRY | Vocal Musical Director

Young Vic includes: *FEAST* (as Musical Director, Arranger and performer).

Other theatre includes: *Barber Shop Chronicles*, *The Amen Corner*, *Emperor and Galilean*, *FELA!*, *Death and the King's Horseman* (National Theatre); *They Drink It in The Congo, Mr Burns* (Almeida); *May Contain Food* (Protein Dance); *Boi Boi is Dead* (West Yorkshire Playhouse); T*he Realness* (The Big House) and *The Merchant of Venice* (The Globe).

Compositions include: Mr. Burns, Boi Boi Is Dead, Circus Tricks, Rocket Symphony, Stand and Birdwatching

Other work includes: *Horrible Histories* for BBC Prom 2011 (as Vocal Animateur and Conductor) and Composer and Choral Director for the 2016 and 2017 Bloomsbury Festival

Mike is a vocalist, composer and arranger in A Capella groups Flying Pickets and The Shout.

AMY BALL CDG | Casting

Previous Young Vic includes: *Feast, The Changeling, Bull, Measure for Measure* and *A Midsummer Night's Dream*.

Other theatre includes: *The Ferryman, Cyprus Avenue, Road* (Royal Court); *Boy* (Almeida Theatre); *Our Ladies of Perpetual Succour* (National Theatre); *The Twits, Linda, How to Hold Your Breath, Hangmen* (Royal Court); *Di and Viv and Rose, Uncle Vanya* (Vaudeville Theatre); *Constellations, Posh* (Duke of York's Theatre); *Jerusalem* (Apollo Theatre) and *Design For Living* (Old Vic).

Amy has been head of casting at the Royal Court Theatre since 2007.

MICHAELA KENNAN | Voice & Dialect

Young Vic includes: *Vernon God Little, The Glass Menagerie, The Government Inspector, The Brothers Size* and *Euridyce*.

Other theatre includes: *Oslo, The Beaux Stratagem, The History Boys* (also West End); *Market Boy, Caroline or Change* (National Theatre); *Everyone's Talking About Jamie* (Apollo and Sheffield Crucible); *Motown The Musical, Memphis The Musical, Hairspray* (Shaftesbury); *Neville's Island* (Duke of York's, Chichester); *South Downs, Browning Version* (Harold Pinter Theatre, Chichester), *Chimerica* (Harold Pinter Theatre, Almeida); *Knives in Hens* (Donmar); *Grounded* (Gate); *The Nether, Routes, Truth & Reconciliation, Love Love Love, The Witness, The Victorian in the Wall* (Royal Court); *The Hypocrite, Hecuba, Oppenheimer* (RSC); *Occupational Hazards* (Hampstead Theatre); *Future Conditional, The Crucible* (Old Vic); *Disgraced, Terre Haute, Artefacts, The Flooded Grave, St Petersburg, The Whiskey Taster* (The Bush).

Opera includes: *Pagliacci* (ENO), *Songs from a Hotel Bedroom* (ROH Linbury Studio).

Television includes: *Dr Who, Odyssey, Grantchester, Midsomer Murders, Millie Imbetween*.

Film includes: *Nine, Cosi, Broken, Omar, Brimstone, Exam*.

TRISTAN FYNN-AIDUENU | Trainee Assistant Director

Training includes: BA in Drama, Theatre and Performance studies with English Literature (First Class Honours, Roehampton University); MA Writing for Stage and Broadcast Media (Central School of Speech and Drama); Young Directors Training Programme (StoneCrabs).

Theatre includes as writer: *Skeen!* (Ovalhouse); *Precious* (Royal Court); *Black Attack* (Bush Theatre); *Sweet Like Chocolate*, *Boy* (Lyric, Cockpit, Ovalhouse); as director: *Little Baby Jesus* (Albany); *Still Barred* (Hackney Showroom) and *Timbuktu* (Arcola).

Tristan is a Creative Associate of the company Initiative.dkf and was an Assistant Producer of the Melanin Box Festival, the first British festival dedicated to blending film, theatre and dance by Black British artists.

LEIAN JOHN-BAPTISTE | Trainee Assistant Director

This is Leian's first time directing for theatre. He is the current Founder and Host of The Plug, a networking platform for aspiring media professionals and Founder and Managing Director of House of Black, a website dedicated to showcasing the work of Black British writers and filmmakers. Previously he was Production Management Assistant at BBC Comedy and Assistant Digital Content Producer at Freeformers.

About The Young Vic

Our shows

We present the widest variety of classics, new plays, forgotten works and music theatre. We tour and co-produce extensively within the UK and internationally.

Our artists

Our shows are created by some of the world's great theatre people, alongside the most adventurous of the younger generation. This fusion makes the Young Vic one of the most exciting theatres in the world.

Our audience

. . . is famously the youngest and most diverse in London. We encourage those who don't think theatre is 'for them' to make it part of their lives. We give 10% of our tickets to schools and neighbours irrespective of box-office demand, and keep prices low.

Our partners near at hand

Each year we engage with over 11,000 local people – individuals and groups of all kinds including schools and colleges – by exploring theatre on and off stage. From time to time we invite our neighbours to appear on our stage alongside professionals.

Our partners further away

By co-producing with leading theatre, opera, and dance companies from London and around the world we create shows neither partner could achieve alone.

The hottest incubator of revitalized classics in London'
The New York Times

'The Young Vic is where theatre magic happens'
Time Out

'Cool, creative, edgy Young Vic'
iNews

'London's most essential theatre'
The Guardian

'Young Vic is London's most lovable theatre. The building welcomes; the programming dares. It offers danger in a safe place'
The Observer

The Young Vic is a company limited by guarantee, registered in England No. 1188209

VAT registration No. 236 673 348

The Young Vic (registered charity number No. 268876) receives public funding from:

Get more from the Young Vic online

/youngvictheatre

@youngvictheatre

/youngviclondon

youngviclondon.wordpress.com

/youngvictheatre

Sign up to receive email updates at
youngvic.org/register

The Young Vic Company

Supporting The Young Vic

To produce our sell-out, award-winning shows and provide thousands of free activities through our Taking Part programme requires major investment. Find out how you can make a difference and get involved.

As an individual . . . become a Friend, donate to a special project, attend our unique gala events or remember the Young Vic in your will.

As a company . . . take advantage of our flexible memberships, exciting sponsorship opportunities, corporate workshops, CSR engagement and venue hire. As a trust or foundation... support our innovative and forward-thinking programmes on stage and off.

As a trust and foundation... support our innovative and forward-thinking programmes on stage and off.

Are you interested in events... hire a space in our award-winning building and we can work with you to create truly memorable workshops, conferences or parties.

For more information visit
youngvic.org/support us
020 7922 2810
Registered charity
(No. 268876)

ACTORS TOURING COMPANY

Actors Touring Company (ATC) makes international, contemporary theatre that travels. We create plays with a global perspective: activating and entertaining the audience while asking questions of the world around us. Placing the performer at the heart of our work, and employing a lean aesthetic which promotes environmental sustainability, the company have toured the UK and internationally since we were founded in 1977, reaching audiences far and wide.

Current and recent productions include: *The Suppliant Women* by Aeschylus in a new version by David Greig, co-produced with the Royal Lyceum Theatre Edinburgh. The production is made to be performed by the community in each place it visits. Most recently co-produced with the Young Vic with a chorus from Lambeth and Southwark, the play will be recreated in March for the Hong Kong Arts Festival and feature a whole new community cast. *Living with the Lights On*, written and performed by Mark Lockyer, about the actor's experience of mental ill health, has toured since 2016, including two runs at the Young Vic as well as at teaching hospitals, secure units and venues as far as Helsinki and Barcelona. A further UK and international tour is planned for 2018. *Winter Solstice* by Roland Schimmelpfennig in co-production with the Orange Tree Theatre, about the rise of the new right across the globe, opened the day after President Trump's inauguration in 2017. *Winter Solstice* will tour the UK in early 2018.

Other recent productions include *The Events*, which has toured extensively in the UK, the US and internationally, and has enjoyed revivals in Denmark, France and Australia.

Actors Touring Company was founded by John Retallack and Dick McCaw in 1977, gaining instant acclaim for an adaptation of Byron's *Don Juan*, then winning a Fringe First in 1978. Subsequently it was resident at the Warehouse Theatre (precursor to the Donmar Warehouse), a regular visitor to the Traverse programme at the Edinburgh Fringe, produced new plays by British writers such as David Grieg, Rebecca Lenkiewicz, Mark Ravenhill, Simon Stephens, Richard Curtis, Nassim Soleimanpour and Bola Agbaje; and UK premieres of new international plays by Roland Schimmelpfennig, Ivan Viripaev and Marius Von Mayenburg.

In 2018, ATC will tour the world – from Europe to South East Asia – and throughout the UK, from Plymouth to Scarborough: just as we have been doing since 1977.

ATC wishes to thank the following
for their generous support of the company

Thistle Trust, Unity Theatre Trust, John and NoraLee Sedmaks, Geraldine Brodie, Alex Stitt, David Lubin,
Christiane Altenburg, Josh Berger, Michael Quine,
Henry Little, Maria Delgado, Patricia Hitchcock, Jo Cottrell,
Stuart Cox, Hilda and Nigel Bellamy, Eleni Gil, Loraine von Moltke.

If you would like to join the Friends of ATC and become
a supporter of our work, please email **atc@atctheatre.com**

atc@atctheatre.com
Facebook: actorstouringcompany
Twitter: @ATCLondon
Instagram: actorstouringcompanyatc

ATC is a registered charity No. 279458

Supported using public funding by
**ARTS COUNCIL
ENGLAND**

Lightning never strikes twice in the same place.
But even so . . .

On a single day in 2006 two friends sent me copies, in typescript, of the same play.

Bijan Sheibani had been my 'assistant' when I directed *As You Like It* in the West End. He'd led a workshop on this play at a smallish London theatre. At week's end, those who ran that theatre hadn't been struck by any special qualities the play might have and had decided it wasn't for them.

By now, Bijan was Artistic Director of the Actors Touring Company. He sent the play to me suggesting that, if I liked it, the Young Vic might care to co-produce it with them.

LATER THE SAME DAY: I open my post. Out of a brown A4 envelope falls a printout of *The Brothers Size – Part of the Brothers/Sisters Plays, by Tarell Alvin McCraney* plus a brief note, written in pencil, from Peter Brook.

'Here's the play I mentioned. You might do something with it.'

I remembered Peter had told me of Tarell. They'd met when Peter had almost directed him (Tarell is/was also an actor) in a revival of one of Peter's big hits *The Suit* in Chicago, a production which I believe didn't actually take place.

In the thirty years I've known Peter, he's only twice sent me a play.

I was about to have some days away.

I can bring to mind exactly where I was when I turned the first page: sprawled out on the grass by a stream in a little valley in France in the bright sun, holding the play up at arm's length over my head to shade my squinting eyes.

In my experience, falling in love is the same with plays as with people: it strikes at once or not at all. I never get to the end of a new play and have to ponder: 'Do I like it or don't I? Shall we go for it or try another from the pile?'

No more than ten pages in to *The Brothers Size* with its curious end-stopped lines – is it verse, is it prose, *what is it exactly*? – I was certain.

I knew. 'I want it. We'll do it.' Then you cross your fingers that the writing stays *that* good all the way to the last page.

And it did. And it still does.

From the first instant you feel that its feet are clad in sturdy, well-fitting boots, it is certain where it's heading, it sets off with a superbly confident stride, it leaps off the path, ambles into the bracken, fords a few rivers, dives into dark woods never breaking step, never losing its thrilling, hurtling poise, its sense of a whole human being on the journey of a lifetime.

Of three whole human beings. Ogun. Oshoosi. Elegba.

I've no idea – I've never asked Tarell – if all or any part of this play channels or reflects or expresses any incident or experience from his own life. As with any art, it's an insolent question. But the sense of particularity – that it could have been written by only one of the billions now walking the earth, by Tarell Alvin McCraney and by no other – beams like a fiery torch from the depths of this remarkable play.

In any world city there ought always to be a theatre where *The Brothers Size* is playing. It's not much to ask. At the Young Vic we're doing our bit. Again with the Actors Touring Company, we're producing it for the third time.

Let that be no more than a beginning. *The Brothers Size* is a lifelong love affair.

David Lan
Artistic Director, Young Vic
2000–2018

Proud to be the lead sponsor of the Funded Ticket Programme

Through IHS Markit's support, the Young Vic offers nearly 10,000 free tickets to young people and many that would not otherwise be able to enjoy the theatre.

 IHS Markit™

Data and Insight for the world's global industries
ihsmarkit.com

TARELL ALVIN McCRANEY

The Brothers Size

FABER & FABER

First published in 2007
by Faber and Faber Limited
74–77 Great Russell Street
London WC1B 3DA

Reprinted 2018

Typeset by Country Setting, Kingsdown, Kent CT14 8ES
Printed in England by CPI Group (UK) Ltd, Croydon CR0 4YY

A CIP record for this book
is available from the British Library

ISBN 978-0-571-34690-5

2 4 6 8 10 9 7 5 3 1

For my brothers, all

Characters

Ogun Henri Size
(OH-GOON)
late twenties, a man of colour, auto mechanic

Oshoosi Size
(O-CHEW-SEE)
early twenties, a man of colour, ex-con,
out on parole, younger brother to Ogun

Elegba
(EH-LEG-BAH)
late twenties, of Creole heritage, also ex-con,
prison mate and best friend of Oshoosi

Setting

San Pere, Louisiana, near the bayou,
distant present

The Brothers Size
draws on elements, icons and stories
from the Yoruba cosmology

THE BROTHERS SIZE

A man that hath friends
must show himself friendly:
and there is a friend that sticketh
closer than a brother.

Proverbs 18: 24

Notes

(Stage directions in parentheses are to be played.)

Other stage directions are to be spoken and played.

Italicised lines indicate songs.

Speech prefixes without following dialogue
are silent actions and hold a rhythm.

Prologue

Lights come up on three men standing on stage. This is the opening invocation and should be repeated for as long as needed to complete the ritual.

Ogun Size
Ogun Size stands in the early morning,
With a shovel in his hand.
He begins his work on the driveway, huh!

Oshoosi Size
Oshoosi Size is in his bed sleeping.
He stirs, dreaming,
A very bad dream, mmm . . .

Elegba
Elegba enters, drifting, like the moon.
Singing a song.

Ogun Size
Sharp breath out.

Elegba
This road is rough . . .

Oshoosi Size
Mmm . . .

Ogun Size
Huh!

Elegba
This road is rough . . .

Oshoosi Size
Mmm . . .

9

Ogun Size
Huh!

Elegba
This road is rough and hard.

Ogun Size
Good God!

Elegba
Its rough and hard . . .

Ogun Size
Lord God!

Elegba
It's rough . . .

Oshoosi Size
Mmm . . .

Ogun Size
Huh!

Elegba
Lord God,
It's rough . . .

Oshoosi Size
Mmm . . .

Ogun Size
Huh!

Elegba
This road is rough,
Yeah, this road is rough . . .

Ogun Size
(sharp breath out)

Act One

Ogun Size
Ogun Size enters.
Osi!

Ogun Size
Calling for his brother
Osi . . .
Oshoosi!

Oshoosi Size
Waking from his dream!
What man, what?

Ogun Size
Get up.

Oshoosi Size
Nigga comin in here turning on lights!

Ogun Size
That's the sun.

Oshoosi Size
Kissing his teeth.

Ogun Size
Oshoosi!

Oshoosi Size
Don't you get tired of going through this?
Every morning we go through this.

Ogun Size
Nigga, get yo ass up!

Oshoosi Size
    This hard?
    Early in the morning you gotta be this hard?

Ogun Size
    Man don't bring me that . . .

Oshoosi Size
    That's your job.
    That car shop got your name, that's your job.

Ogun Size
    Where your job?

Oshoosi Size
    I ain't got none.
    I am currently seeking employment.

Ogun Size
    Currently?

Oshoosi Size
    I'm tired!

Ogun Size
    So you just gone lay up here today?

Oshoosi Size
    Yeah, buddy.
    I don't sleep good at night, and
    Tossed and turned all this morning.
    Tired, brother.

Ogun Size
    Kisses teeth.

Oshoosi Size
    Yeah man, you should stay home.

Ogun Size
    The shop, man . . .

Oshoosi Size
Ogun, you better stop, man.
Stop doing it to yourself.
You keep working like that,
Every day all day at that damn shop,
You gone work yourself to death, man.
You better don't . . .
Death kill the lazy last.

Ogun Size
Stop working?

Oshoosi Size
Nah . . . rest.
Get you some ass.

Ogun Size
Quit working?

Oshoosi Size
You own the car shop, yeah?
That car shop yours.
Say Ogun's Carshack, right?

Ogun Size
Yeah . . .

Oshoosi Size
You ain't got to quit, just get somebody to work it
for you.

Ogun Size
Deal.

Oshoosi Size
What?

Ogun Size
You hired.

Oshoosi Size
Nigga!

Ogun Size
You ain't got no job, right . . .

Oshoosi Size
You know . . .

Ogun Size
You 'currently seeking employment . . .'

Oshoosi Size
Ogun . . .

Ogun Size
Seek yo ass into that truck in five minutes.

Oshoosi Size
I ain't applied for this job,
I ain't even knowed you was hiring . . .

Ogun Size
You more than qualified, brother.

Oshoosi Size
Ah come on, Og.

Ogun Size
Effective today, Osi.

Oshoosi Size
Nah man, nah, I'm turning this shit down.
I don't want your job.

Ogun Size
Wait a minute . . .

Oshoosi Size
Oh shit . . .

Ogun Size
You turning down work?

Oshoosi Size
Shit.

Ogun Size
Oh man, you turning down a lot of shit.
First off you forfeit your living here rights . . .

Oshoosi Size
You threatening me?

Ogun Size
I promise you.

Oshoosi Size
Fuck that!
I'll stay with Aunt Ele!

Ogun Size
Gua ain't gone put up with your shit!
Ele Gua ain't never like us and fo sure not you.
You also forcing me to tell your parole officer
You won't work.
Smiles.
Ogun Size exits.

Oshoosi Size
Are you . . .
Fo real . . .
This nigga!

Ogun Size
From outside:
Beep!

Oshoosi Size
I swear fore God . . .
I swear this nigga . . .
Got the working love, man.
Shit.
Know a nigga don't feel like no

Getting up he come in here.
'Oshoosi . . .'
Like my name slave,
Like my name on that damn car shop . . .
'Oshoosi.'
That even . . .
He like that shit,
Up all early in the morning working,
For what?
On what?
Nigga need to get up and build me a damn car.
A nigga need to get around.
How I'm supposed to get a girl,
Pick up, walk round on my feet?
Feet already flat.

Ogun Size
Beep!

Oshoosi Size
You hold the hell on!
Black bastard.
If I am going to work I'm a' smell G-double-O-D good.
Can't be workin and smelling like yo ass . . .
Always funky.
Nigga stay dirty!
He ain't even that black.
I was always darker than him.
Everybody know that . . .
Damn shoe . . .
Everybody know I was darker cause of my daddy.
His daddy was red.
Redder than Mama.
He walking around here . . .

Ogun Size
Beep!

Oshoosi Size
    Keep on, Og!
    Keep on, Ogun.
    Keep on the way you do.
    Every beep I'm a' take even longer to get dressed.
    Going in there to get oil all on me n' shit.
    You think I'm gone hurry up for that?
    That nigga threaten to tell my parole!
    He supposed to be my brother . . .
    That . . .
    He . . .
    Boy, I swear you can't win . . .
    Not round here . . .
    Huh!

Ogun Size
    Coming back in,
    Osi!

Oshoosi Size
    Eh, man . . .

Ogun Size
    Boy, put that damn cologne down!

Oshoosi Size
    Look!

Ogun Size
    Get cha ass in the car!

Oshoosi Size
    Laughing:
    Something-to-myself-cause-I-don't-want-you-to-hear-
        cause-it's-for-me.

Ogun Size
    What cha say?
    Say it again.

Oshoosi Size
Mumbling, man.
I don't want to hurt your feelings.

Ogun Size
Huh.
Eh!
Don't slam my truck . . .

Oshoosi Size
Outside.
Slam!

Ogun Size
Bastard!

SCENE TWO

Oshoosi Size
Oshoosi Size on lunch break,
Drinking a Coke Cola,
Singing a song.
(*Sings a song.*)

Elegba
Elegba enters, drifting, like the moon . . .
Sang that song, nigga!

Oshoosi Size
Huh? Eh, Legba!

Elegba
You sing, nigga, and the angels stop humming . . .

Oshoosi Size
You crazy.

Elegba
It's true, brother!

Where you get a voice like that?
I been wondering since lock-up,
'How Oshoosi get his voice?'

Oshoosi Size

Ah hell, Legba, you got a voice.

Elegba

But my voice clear,
I know that, I was born a choirboy.
But you? You a siren.

Oshoosi Size

What?

Elegba

A siren!
You ope up your mouth an' everybody know where
    the pain at.
Your voice come out and say, 'The pain right here.
It's here, see it? See?'

Oshoosi Size

C'mon, man . . .

Elegba

You don't like nobody to brag on you . . .

Oshoosi Size

Nah, man.

Elegba

That's alright. I ain't scared to,
Everybody needs somebody to brag on him.
You like my brother, man . . . I ain't scared to brag
    on you.
Ain't embarrassed about my brother.
Nah, too cool to be embarrassed.

Oshoosi Size

My man Legba!

Elegba
I see Og got you round here workin.

Oshoosi Size
Lookin like a grease monkey.

Elegba
You shouldn'ta told him.

Oshoosi Size
Shit, really I didn't tell him.

Elegba
Nah?

Oshoosi Size
Hell nah.

Elegba
You didn't tell him that we worked on cars locked up?

Oshoosi Size
He ask what we do in the pen.
I say, 'Wait, mutha . . .'
That's what we do.
Man, sometimes he ask dumb-ass questions.
He ask me what we do in the pen.
'Wait.
Cry.
Wait.'

Elegba
You right.

Oshoosi Size
I say, 'Work and wait.'
He say, 'Work?'
I say, 'Work . . .
Cry,
Shit,
Pray, nigga.
What you think?'

Elegba
What he say to that?

Oshoosi Size
He look at me and say, 'Work, huh?'

Elegba
That's it.

Oshoosi Size
I'm here.

Elegba
You shouldn'ta told him everything.

Oshoosi Size
I spoke it all, man.

Elegba
You say it all?
All about the pen?

Oshoosi Size

Elegba

Oshoosi Size
Nah, I ain't tell him all that.

Elegba
Yeah, that shit ain't nothin.

Oshoosi Size
Nah. Hell, nah.
The pen got me dreamin about pussy nightly.

Elegba
Man . . .

Oshoosi Size
Had to hold your own self tight at night.

Elegba
You didn't, won't nobody to do it for you.

Oshoosi Size
Nah. Hell, nah.
Nigga's always offerin.

Elegba
Or trying to take it.

Oshoosi Size
That shit crazy, crazy shit.
I didn't think they would get like that.

Elegba
Man, when you in need your mind . . .

Oshoosi Size
Man . . .
Sometimes I had to remind myself,
That I wouldn't gone be there that long.

Elegba
Yeah, you only had a year.

Oshoosi Size
Two.

Elegba
Lucky nigga.

Oshoosi Size
Ah nigga, you got out right after me.

Elegba
Eh man, we went at the same time, came out same time.
We got close like that.
Helped each other.

Oshoosi Size
Yeah, man.

Elegba
We was like brothers.

Oshoosi Size
Yeah.

Elegba
Brothers in need.

Ogun Size
Ogun enters covered in oil!

Elegba
Og!

Ogun Size
Niggas!

Oshoosi Size
Why you got to be so hard all the time?

Ogun Size
You need something, Legba?
I didn't see no car?

Elegba
Nah, Og, just came to see my brother.

Ogun Size
Where he at?

Elegba
Ah, Size Number One, you know how we call each
    other brothers.

Ogun Size
Pissed at being called
Size Number One,
Yeah, I know how.
Osi, get that part I asked you for.

Elegba
Well, I guess I be going . . .

Oshoosi Size
Take it easy, Legba.

Elegba
Oh man, you know . . .

Ogun Size
Yeah, you be easy, Legba.
Bring a car next time you come through.
Give me something to do while you brothers
Conversate . . .

Elegba
Converse.

Ogun Size

Elegba
Elegba exits the way he came.

Ogun Size

Oshoosi Size
Why you always got to . . .

Ogun Size
I asked you for that part almost ten . . .

Oshoosi Size
Man, I took a break.

Ogun Size
Your ass couldn't've told me that
Before I was getting oil in my eyes!

Oshoosi Size
That's a good colour on you.

Ogun Size
Playin, that's what you always doin.

Oshoosi Size
Man, I was being cordial.

Ogun Size
You don't need to be nice to that nigga.

Oshoosi Size
That's my friend.

Ogun Size
You don't make no friends in the pen.

Oshoosi Size
What you know?

Ogun Size
Bring the part, Osi.

Oshoosi Size
'Bring the part, Osi.'

Elegba
Elegba returns.
Eh . . .

Oshoosi Size
Oh you back, man?
I gotta get to work.

Elegba
Nah, nah, I know.
But um, listen.
You got a ride?

Oshoosi Size
Nah, not yet.

Elegba
Your brotha the king a' cars
And you ain't got no ride?

Oshoosi Size
Ain't that the shit?

Elegba

You sayin it, man.
As much as you talked about getting a ride when we
was locked up . . .

Oshoosi Size

Yeah! Right.

Elegba

All that talk about how riding is the ultimate freedom.
Every other word out yo mouth was about a car . . .
Remember?

Oshoosi Size

I know . . .

Elegba

Brother, you talked about cars so much,
I was scared for you to get out cause I swore
The first thing you was gone do was go out and steal
you one.

Oshoosi Size

Shut up, Legba . . .

Elegba

I'm just saying, man . . .
Remember all you talk about was a car?
I say that nigga gone get him a car.
And you ain't got no car yet.
Man, please how that work?

Oshoosi Size

I hear you, Legba.

Elegba

I'm just saying, man.
You know me. I don't mean nothing.
Talk too much and too slow.

Oshoosi Size
Nah, you alright, brother.

Elegba
Well, I will let you get back.
I gotta get to work too.

Oshoosi Size
You got a job, nigga?

Elegba
Working at the funeral home.

Oshoosi Size
Hell to the nah.

Elegba
Yeah, it's paying good,
It's alright . . .

Oshoosi Size
Legba man, you working
On dead people.

Elegba
Better than working with live people.
This way nobody don't bother me.

Oshoosi Size
I don't like the look of the dead.

Elegba
You gone be dead some day too.

Oshoosi Size
Yeah, but I don't need yo ass to remind me.

Elegba
It's good to remember . . .
So you know you need to do now,
So you know that you ain't got forever, just right now.
Good to remember death, man.

Oshoosi Size
I guess I hear you.

Elegba
Eh,
Osi, man.
I ain't mean to bring you down.

Oshoosi Size
Nah, man, I'm alright . . .

Elegba
Eh, see about that car, Oshoosi.

Oshoosi Size
Yeah. Yeah . . .

Elegba
You my brother, man.

Oshoosi Size
Eh, man . . . I know that.

Elegba
Lay it down . . .
Elegba offers his hand to Oshoosi.

Oshoosi Size
Oshoosi takes it, how could he not?
You alright, man.

SCENE THREE

Ogun Size
Ogun Size goes under the car.

Oshoosi Size
Ogun . . .

Ogun Size
What?

Oshoosi Size
I need a ca . . .

Ogun Size
Coming from under the car,
Holding a part, irritated.
What?

Oshoosi Size
Um . . . what does that part do?

Ogun Size
Sighs . . . ignoring his baby brother.
I'm trying to concentrate!
Goes back under car.

Oshoosi Size
How long you think before you retire?

Ogun Size
I just started . . .

Oshoosi Size
Yeah but shit, you doing good, brother.

Ogun Size
Huh.

Oshoosi Size
Hey, Og . . .

Ogun Size
Ogun comes from under the car.
Nigga, they let you talk this much in the pen?
Ogun goes back under the car.

Oshoosi Size
Oshoosi kicks at his brother.

Ogun Size
Ogun comes from under the car.

Oshoosi Size
Oshoosi smiles innocently.

Ogun Size
Ogun goes back under the car.

Oshoosi Size

Ogun Size

Oshoosi Size

Ogun Size

Oshoosi Size
Man, I need some pussy.

Ogun Size
Bang.
Shit!

Oshoosi Size
And the way you running into shit you need some too.
When was the last time you had some good coochie?

Ogun Size
Comes from the under the car.
Coo? Did you say coochie?
When was the last time *you* had some?

Oshoosi Size
Nigga, you know the answer to that!
I ain't been out but a minute.
Shit, seen more you than I seen myself.
You know I ain't had nothing for a minute.
Man, but when I do . . . Boy, looka here.
BLOCKA!

Ogun Size
Looks at Oshoosi like
'What the fuck?'

Oshoosi Size
BLOCKA! BLOCKA!

Ogun Size
Shakes his head.

Oshoosi Size

Ogun Size
Ogun goes back under the car.

Oshoosi Size
BLOCKA!
Eh, Og . . .
Og, whatever happened to Oya?
Huh. That girl had a thing for you.
Man, she had a thing for you.
She loved her some Ogun Size.
In school I remember, you was in high school,
And we go to the meets and she blow you a kiss while
    she burning it up on that track.
She was so phyne, black as night, almost black as that
    asphalt – all that ass!
All them legs like a Clydesdale legs. Sweet girl, Oya.
Run like the wind.
Whatever happened to her?

Ogun Size
She was wit my boy Shango.
She stop talking to me . . . started seeing him.

Oshoosi Size
Oh.
Man, I'm
Sorry, I didn't know, that's fucked up . . .

Ogun Size
You know him, right? Basketball team.
Go through women like draws . . . He in the army now.
Shango, my best friend . . . Huh.

He say to Oya, he walk to her one day, he say, 'You
   should be with me.
Ogun ain't going nowhere. You should be with me.'
Guess it sound sweet to her.
She start seeing him, talking to him.
But he got other girls he seeing . . .
He come into town for furlough or whatever and he
   come to see 'em one by one.
He pay Oya some attention sometimes . . .
See her sometimes
I used to see her walking around, got this sad-ass look
   on her face . . . like she sick.
She ain't sick, just sad.
Sad like that after-rain breeze . . . just sad.
I wanna grab her, sometimes, when I would see her,
I wanna grab and hold her so bad.
But she ain't mine no more.
She with that nigga . . . she with him.
I ain't say nothing . . . just respect that that's that
   man's girl.
She grown she in her own situation.
You know . . . She . . .
Shango had this other girl . . . guess it's his main girl.
Shun . . . She . . . man, she beautiful . . . Shun.
Beautiful.
All the niggas I know want her . . .

Oshoosi Size
Yeah, I know Shun.

Both
Evil bitch . . .

Ogun Size
She ain't neva been wrong to me. Always say, 'Hey
   Ogun, how you doin?' But she got that way about her.
   You know how she smiling but you know she think
   you beneath her. One of them kind. So she tells Oya

she pregnant with Shango's baby. Just walked up to Oya with them hips, you know, and was like, 'My name Shun, I got his baby so you ain't shit to him.' And see, Oya can't have no kids. Everybody know that. Now she scared she gone lose Shango. Which would be good if she left the nigga . . . But she can't see that, nah, she got to show him how much she willing to do for Shango. How far she willing to go for Shango. So she can't give him no child, she cut off her ear.

Oshoosi Size
What!

Ogun Size
Put it in a bowl and walked it to him while he was watching TV at her house. She ain' scream, uh nothing . . .
Cut off her ear and gave it to him. Say, 'I don't want nobody but you.' Say, 'This mark me as yours . . . Nobody else want me they see this.'
Shango left her ass there bleeding. Call her a crazy bitch, say she sick. She wasn't sick . . . just sad. Sad. She sitting like a lake up in the home they put her in . . . laying on her back holding her head staring at the sky.
You look at her you, you think she floating somewhere. Oya. Beautiful fast Oya. Sad girl.

Oshoosi Size
Man, that's some Van Gogh shit right there.

Ogun Size

Oshoosi Size

Ogun Size
What you know?

Oshoosi Size
What I . . .

Ogun Size
Can't talk to you bout shit.

Oshoosi Size
What I say?

Ogun Size
Nothing, just being you, nothing.
Nigga been outta jail all of five minutes
Think he know all.
Ogun goes back under the car.

SCENE FOUR

Ogun Size
Dinner.
Unusually quiet.
Eating.

Oshoosi Size
Eating.

Ogun Size
What you up to?

Oshoosi Size
Eatin my dinner . . .

Ogun Size
I wanna know now, Os.

Oshoosi Size
Nigga?

Ogun Size
Tell me . . .

Oshoosi Size
What's wrong wit you?

Ogun Size
You ain't never this quiet.

Oshoosi Size
I'm hungry . . . I'm tired . . .

Ogun Size
Hungry?
You eatin leftovers!

Oshoosi Size
Eh, I ain't ingrateful . . .

Ogun Size
That's the point, you are.
You don't do nothing quiet –
You snore loud as hell,
You moan when you piss,
And when you eat you talk more
Shit than you chew!
You up to something, I don't know what it is,
Oshoo, but you better tell me now.
Cause if I find out you doing some . . .

Oshoosi Size
Damn, boy, I swear . . .

Ogun Size
I'm not gone run to your rescue . . .

Oshoosi Size
Can't have no peace.

Ogun Size
You think, 'Ogun gone get me outta this,'
You can forget that shit . . .
Don't do something to put your ass back in the pen!

Oshoosi Size
  What?

Ogun Size
  I said . . .

Oshoosi Size
  Eh man, you want to go to jail, Og?
  Tell me, let me know, I am sure I can arrange something.
  Cause you mention that shit bout every five fucking
    minutes . . .
  I been home but two, three months . . .
  In that time I swear you ain't let me forget once that
    I, at one time, was not free . . .
  Why you got to be so hard all the goddamn time?
  I'm the one who should be walking around like a
    stone, man . . .
  You act like you in jail . . .
  You in jail, Og? Hmm . . .?
  Something holding you down, Ogun?
  If that's it you need to loose that shit and run, man . . .
  Before you become rock.
  I ain't doin nothing . . .
  Just trying to live easy, man . . .
  Damn . . . it's gone be like this?
  Let me know . . .
  Let me know now cause I will get my shit,
  Get my shit and go . . .
  But while I am here . . .
  Man, you let me be free . . .
  I got enough memories to wash out without you
  Putting in a fresh supply every five minutes . . .
  That shit ain't right . . .
  It ain't right, man . . .
  It ain't.

Ogun Size

Oshoosi Size

Ogun Size

Oshoosi Size

Ogun Size

Oshoosi Size
  Goes back to eating.

Ogun Size

Oshoosi Size
  Eating.

Ogun Size
  Eating.

Oshoosi Size
  Eh man, I need a ride . . .

Ogun Size
  I knew it!
  Knew you were . . .

Oshoosi Size
  Nigga, you the king of cars . . .

Ogun Size
  You lookin around here?
  I ain't the king of shit.
  Kings don't come home greased from
  The knees down.

Oshoosi Size
  Eh, every man's castle ain't in England, man.
  Every man's palace ain't made of sand
  And gold and shit.
  Your palace made out of them cars, Og.
  You put cars back together better than any nigga cross
    this place.
  You the regent to come to about a car.

Ogun Size
What you need a car for?
You ain't got no job to go to.

Oshoosi Size
That ain't what I'm talking about.
You know what I am talking about?
You pushing the conversation somewhere else!
We talking about cars, man.
I need a ride.
I want to drive somewhere . . .

Ogun Size
Where?
Yo ass still on probation.

Oshoosi Size
Damn it, son of a bitch!

Ogun Size
Watch your mouth.

Oshoosi Size
I know I am still on probation!
I know, Og.
Damn!
I know I was once in prison.
I am out and I am on probation.
Damn it, man.
I ain't trying to drive to Fort Knox.
I ain't about to scale the Capitol . . .
I want a ride.
I want to drive out to the bayou . . .
Maybe take a lady down there . . .
And relax . . .
Shit, what if I just wanted to go by myself?
What if I wanted to be there alone?
What difference it make?
Damn.

You can't fathom that?
You can't fit that round yo big-ass head?
You trying to lock me up again?
You trying to make my feet stuck?
Stuck here, in here . . .
Well, you just give me the word, Og.
Tell me now like a man you want me to be miserable.
Fuck the car . . .
Mention prison again . . .
Make mention of it like you do . . .
That shit stops now.
I mean that.
I done served my time, Ogun.
Sentence complete.
Done.
Done.
You sleep good tonight.
I won't.

SCENE FIVE

Oshoosi Size
Oshoosi Size is sleeping, that night, dreaming.
And in his dream is his brother Ogun.
Oshoosi can hear him, in this dream, working,
On something, on what?

Ogun Size
Huh!

Oshoosi Size
Oshoosi is sleeping, dreaming.
Dreaming a sad dream and in his dream, enters
Elegba too. Singing a sweet song.

Elegba
Mmm hmm.

Ogun Size
Huh.

Elegba
Mmm hmm.

Ogun Size
Huh.

Elegba
Oshoosi Size.

Ogun Size
Huh.

Elegba
Cell number . . .

Ogun Size
Huh.

Elegba
Inmate number.

Ogun Size
Huh.

Elegba
Oshoosi,
Oshoosi Size.
You remember?
Don't you?
Those late nights . . .

Ogun Size
Huh.

Elegba
So hot.

Oshoosi Size
So hot.

Elegba
When the walls come closer,
Closer . . .
At night.
Night . . .

Ogun Size
Huh.

Elegba
Deep night . . .
That's when it most dangerous . . .
Cause sometimes in the night . . .

Oshoosi Size
Night.

Ogun Size
Huh.

Elegba
You don't know what come for you, wei?

Ogun Size
Huh.

Elegba
You know not where the hand will lead you.

Ogun Size
Huh.

Elegba
If it's the good guard lead you back to your cell . . .

Ogun Size
Huh.

Elegba
If it ain't . . .

Ogun Size
Huh.

Elegba
You remember?
Me your friend . . .
Like your brother?

Ogun Size
Huh.

Elegba
Your brother in need.
I remember you . . . in there with me.
We were down in there sleepwalking together.
Got so I could tell when you wanted to eat without
You saying it . . . tell when you wanted to piss or sleep
Or . . .

Ogun Size
Huh.

Oshoosi Size
Mmm.

Elegba
I know you scared . . .

Oshoosi Size
Scared

Elegba
I know you in that place.

Ogun Size
Huh.

Elegba
Prison make grown men scared of the dark again.
Put back the boogy-monsters and the voodoo man
We spend our whole life trying to forget . . .

Ogun Size
Huh.

Elegba
You scared.

Oshoosi Size
Scared . . .

Elegba
I know you are . . .

Ogun Size
Huh.

Oshoosi Size
Dark.

Elegba
But I am here in the dark . . .
I come for you like I always do . . .

Ogun Size
Huh.

Elegba
In that night hour when you know nobody else
Around . . . Legba come down and sing for you . . .

Ogun Size
Huh.

Elegba
You sing with me?
Mmm.

Oshoosi Size
Mmm.

Elegba
Yeah, we sing so we know we together . . .

Ogun Size
Huh.

Elegba
You and me make it so our harmony make a light . . .

Ogun Size
Huh.

Elegba
Light on the earth and the air . . .
You and me.

Ogun Size
Huh.

Elegba
In the dark.
I know you in that dark place . . .
Where no one else knows you.
You don't have to be scared no more . . .

Oshoosi Size
Mmm.

Elegba
Mmm.

Elegba *and* **Oshoosi Size**
Mmm.

Elegba
Don't cry.
Don't cry . . .
I will walk you through,
Take you lightly into the night.
Make you smile.
Open your hand and smile.
That M&M kind of smile.

Oshoosi Size
    Hah.

Elegba
    It's funny ain't it, Osi . . .?
    Huh.
    Funny.
    Oshoosi Size . . .
    My brother . . .
    Can you walk with me?
    I am your taker.
    I am here to take you home.
    Just when you thought you walked alone.
    I am here.

Ogun Size
    Osi . . .

Elegba
    Here.

Ogun Size
    Osi.

Elegba
    Here.

Ogun Size *and* **Elegba**
    Osi!

SCENE SIX

Oshoosi Size
    Oshoosi Size wakes from a nightmare.
    Realising, ah hell, he late for work.

Oshoosi Size
Oshoosi Size begins walking to work!

Ogun Size
STEP!

Elegba
STEP!

Ogun Size
Step.

Elegba
Step.

Oshoosi Size
Hot sun on my back,
Hot in my face!
Hot.

Elegba
Step.

Ogun Size
Step.

Elegba
Step.

Ogun Size
Step.

Oshoosi Size
Making me walk
Through this hot-ass sun!
Man!

Ogun Size
Step.

Elegba
Step.

Ogun Size
Step.

Elegba
Step on.

Oshoosi Size
He . . .
You know he can be . . .
He better be . . .

Elegba
Step on.

Ogun Size
Just step on.

Oshoosi Size
Why he left, though?
He act like I wouldn't
Just gone go back to bed.
Just lay my ass down . . .

Elegba
Step.

Ogun Size
Step on . . .

Oshoosi Size
I would've . . .
Sure as hell should've . . .
Laid my black ass right back down . . .
Left my damn keys in the house.
Door locked.
Now I got to . . .
This sun!
Fucking car shop.

Walking.
Ogun!

Elegba
Step on.

Ogun Size *and* **Elegba**
Just step on.

Oshoosi Size
Nigga.
You wait til I see Ogun Henri Size!
I'm, ah . . .
Boy!
I standing my ground today.
I'm cutting ties this afternoon.
I swear that.
Step.

Ogun Size
Step.

Elegba
Step.

Ogun Size
Step on.

Elegba
Step on.

Ogun Size
Just step on.

Elegba
Step.

Oshoosi Size
Well, it's hard.

Elegba
It's hard.

Oshoosi Size
Lord Almighty.

Ogun Size
Step.

Oshoosi Size
It's hard.

Elegba
It's hard.

Oshoosi Size
Lord Almighty.

Elegba
Mighty.

Ogun Size
Step.

Oshoosi Size
Say it's hard.

Elegba
It's hard.

Oshoosi Size
Lord Almighty!

Ogun Size
Step.

Oshoosi Size
Come on, Lord.

Elegba
A wella.

Oshoosi Size
Well, I ain't been to Georgy Georgy . . .

Elegba
Well.

Oshoosi Size
But I been told.

Elegba
A wella.

Oshoosi Size
I ain't been to Georgy Georgy.

Elegba
Well.

Oshoosi Size
But I been told –

Elegba
A wella.

Oshoosi Size
That them sweet Georgia girls –

Ogun Size, Elegba *and* **Oshoosisize**
Lord Amighty.

Oshoosi Size
They make a man wanna die.

Elegba
A wella.

Oshoosi Size
Well, it's hard . . .

Elegba
It's hard.

Oshoosi Size
Lord Almighty.

Ogun Size
Step.

Oshoosi Size
It's hard.

Elegba
It's hard.

Oshoosi Size
Lord Almighty mighty.

Ogun Size
Step.

Oshoosi Size
It's hard.

Elegba
It's hard.

Oshoosi Size
Lord Almighty.

Ogun Size, Elegba *and* **Oshoosisize**
Come on, boys, a wella.

SCENE EIGHT

Oshoosi Size
Oshoosi at the shop!
Standing breathing hard
From the walk.

Ogun Size
Glad you could make it

Oshoosi Size

Ogun Size
Can you bring a box from the . . .

Oshoosi Size
Stares at his brother . . .

Ogun Size
You here now no need to be . . .

Oshoosi Size
  You left me.

Ogun Size
  You overslept.

Oshoosi Size
  You wake me up every morning . . .

Ogun Size
  You . . .

Oshoosi Size
  You left me there . . .
  I ain't come here to work.
  I quit.

Ogun Size
  You fired.

Oshoosi Size
  All the better.
  I will pack my shit.

Ogun Size
  You don't have to leave.

Oshoosi Size
  I don't want to hear your shit, Og, you know
  I don't.

Ogun Size
  You can stay.
  Just find a job.

Oshoosi Size
  I planned to.

Ogun Size
  Then we square, brother.

Oshoosi Size
  You left me.

Ogun Size
  I know.

Oshoosi Size
  That's fucked up.

Ogun Size
  Huh.
  You don't want me to treat you like you locked up
    no mo.
  What you say last night, Osi?
  You say don't tell me when to and what to do no more.
  I listen.
  I'm listening . . .

Oshoosi Size
  You left me.

Ogun Size
  So you got to get up when you got up.

Oshoosi Size
  Interrupts.
  I looked around and you was gone.

Ogun Size
  Not when nobody else tell you.

Oshoosi Size
  I walked here . . .

Ogun Size
  You can't get up lessen you want to, no way.

Oshoosi Size
  It was hot.

Ogun Size
  I can't get up for you.

Oshoosi Size
  I'll see you at the house.

Ogun Size
Yeah.
Realising . . .
You walked?

Elegba
Elegba enters.

Elegba *and* **Oshoosi Size**
Hell, yeah!

Oshoosi Size
Hot as hell out there.

Elegba
Breathing hard . . .

Oshoosi Size
What's up, Legba?

Elegba
I had to push her here . . .

Ogun Size
Push who?
Who you pushed?

Elegba
I had to push her most of the way . . .
She wouldn't go up on me . . .

Ogun Size
What you talking about?

Oshoosi Size
A realisation.
A car.

Elegba
A car.

Ogun Size
A car?
Where?

Elegba
She down there.
I couldn't get her up that hill.

Oshoosi Size
Hell, I barely made it up that hill.

Ogun Size
But you made it.

Elegba
Me and no car wasn't gone make it.

Oshoosi Size
Excited as hell!
A car!

Elegba
Can you look at her, Og?

Ogun Size
You got money?

Oshoosi Size
Eh!

Ogun Size
What?

Elegba
I can pay you tell me what's wrong.

Ogun Size
Down the hill?
Will it start?

Elegba
Yeah.

Ogun Size
    Ogun exits.

Oshoosi Size
    Sorry about that.

Elegba
    What?

Oshoosi Size
    Him, man, he can be hard sometimes.

Elegba
    It's alright.
    You got a car?

Oshoosi Size
    Nah.

Elegba
    Take this one.

Oshoosi Size
    What you mean, man?

Elegba

Oshoosi Size
    What you doing?

Elegba
    Nothing!

Oshoosi Size
    Why you giving me a car?

Elegba
    Well, I ain't giving it to you . . .

Oshoosi Size
    Where it come from?

Elegba
I found it.

Oshoosi Size
Nigga!
C'mon, Legba, you found a car?

Elegba
In my cousin's dump.

Oshoosi Size
What I'm a do with a car that don't work?

Ogun Size
Excited, breathing heavy.
It's fine . . .

Elegba
It's fine . . .

Oshoosi Size
It's fine?

Ogun Size
Better than fine.
That car in good shape.
The outside beat up . . .
But even that's a cool blue,
All you got to do is polish that up.
You ain't have no problems with cars like that . . .
Yeah, you got to tune it up sometimes . . .
Pop it when it's buckin on you,
But those one of those American classics.
Those, 'I will run longer and stronger then the human
    body' cars. Man, please, that car got plenty run in it.

Oshoosi Size
Why Legba couldn't get her to run?

Elegba
I ain't got no licence.

Oshoosi Size
Nigga, you don't know how to drive?

Elegba
I mean I do.
I think I do still remember.
But my licence still suspended.
Gotta get a new one.
Beside, I ran into the law the other day.

Oshoosi Size
Oh shit.

Ogun Size
Ah nah.

Elegba
Yeah.

Oshoosi Size
What he say?

Ogun Size
He say something to you?

Elegba
What he always say?

All
'Eh, boy.'

Ogun Size
'What you doing round here?'

Oshoosi Size
'Stay out of the shit for you start to stink.'

Elegba
'What you doing?
Where you going?
Better be quick.'

Ogun Size
I swear that man ain't neva gone change.

Oshoosi Size
Anytime he see another black man in
Town he act like he got to chase him out.

Elegba
Sheriff act like he the only nigga
Can be seen in the town.

Oshoosi Size
He ask you questions too, Og?

Ogun Size
Man, you know he treat everybody like
We guilty till proven innocent.

Elegba
Cept them white folks.

Oshoosi Size
Nothing but, 'How do, sir.'

Ogun Size
'Morning.'

Elegba
'Morning, sir.
Y'all might want take shed of this sun lessen
You want to get as dark as me today,
Ha ha ha!'

Oshoosi Size
And they laugh too.

Elegba
Yeah, they do.

Ogun Size
Laugh with the darkie play-play-sheriff.

Oshoosi Size
Laugh, nigga, laugh.

Ogun Size
'Lessen you want to get as dark as me.'

Elegba
He see me see him.

Oshoosi Size
Huh?

Elegba
He see me look his way on the way to the Food Lion.
He look over his glasses.

Ogun Size
That smile just coming off his face, I bet.

Elegba
The white people he talking to walk on by,
Some of the Witt boys,
They walk on by . . .
But he stay there looking at me.

Oshoosi Size
He had you in sights.

Ogun Size
You caught him playing monkey.

Oshoosi Size
That's a crime in itself.

Ogun Size
Punishable by death.

Elegba
He say, 'Where you going, Legba?'

Oshoosi Size
He remember your name?

Ogun Size
He call me Size.

Oshoosi Size
Call me Size too.

Ogun Size
Like we twins . . .

Oshoosi Size
Or the same person.

Ogun Size
Like it's only one of us.

Oshoosi Size
Like we the same.

Elegba
'Where you going, Legba?'
'Nowhere, sir.'
Huh.

Oshoosi Size
Huh.

Ogun Size
Huh.

Elegba
'When they let you out?'

Oshoosi Size
Let you?

Elegba
'They didn't let me do nothing.
I served my time.
Did all of it.
Got a job work at the funeral home.'

Ogun Size
Legba, you work at the . . .

Oshoosi Size
Leave it lone, Ogun.

Elegba
'You got you a job, huh, boy?
You think you fully rehabitulated, son?'

Ogun Size
What?

Elegba
You know, 'rehabitulated'.

Oshoosi Size
What the fuck is that?

Elegba
Ha, the nigga trying to say 'rehabilitated'.

Oshoosi Size
Niggas.

Ogun Size
Stupid nigga.

Elegba
'You fully rehabitulated?'
'Yes, sir, I think I am.'
'You think?'
'I think, sir.'
'You should know, shouldn't you?'
'I guess.'
'There you go again, son, guessing, thinking . . .
That's what got you in trouble in the first place,
    ain't it?
Thinking you was too fast.
Thinking you could get away . . .

If you was better, you would know better than to
Think or guess ever again.'

Oshoosi Size

What you say, Legba?

Ogun Size

What you say?

Elegba

I say, 'Maybe you right, sir.'
'Maybe!'

Ogun Size

Oh no.

Oshoosi Size

Shit, Legba.

Elegba

'Maybe I'm right, huh?
Well, let's go see your parole officer see if he think
    I'm right.'
'What fo?'
'Well, you bout to go back in, ain't you?'
'Why!'
'You standing here loitering.'
'No, sir.'
'You ain't, no?
Well you got a clear answer to that.'
'Yes, sir.'
'Don't let me catch you running, Legba.'
'Sir?'
'Don't stand still and don't run . . .
Don't wanna see you riding or flying . . .
Every time I see you I better see you
Getting where you need to go,
Where you should be going,
The way God intended for you to get there,

Before the modern inventions of life made it
Easier for the scum of the earth to transport they
  evil deeds.
Back when all you had was your feet to the earth . . .
Don't let your transgressions vine up around you,
  son . . .'

Oshoosi Size
'Don't let the weeds of the world strangle you.'

Ogun Size
'The mud . . .'

Elegba
'Don't let it stick you and choke you.
Don't play in the shit, you'll start to stink.'
'Yes, sir.'

Oshoosi Size
'Yes, sir.'

Ogun Size
Huh.

Elegba
That's when the Witt boys came back.
Asked him if they could have a ride half back to the
  house.
They say they taken his advice trying not to catch
  sunstroke
Walking back home.
'You good boys, come on, catch a ride.'
Smiling.

Oshoosi Size
Beaming, huh.

Ogun Size
Big smile.

Elegba

That M&M kind of smile.

Oshoosi Size

Oshoosi stares at Elegba
Like someone who just heard
A ghost or remembered a dream.

Elegba

You know, like they just asked to blow sunshine up
his ass.

Ogun Size

Might do.

Oshoosi Size

Huh.

Elegba

So I decided to push her over rather than risk getting
caught riding.

Oshoosi Size

Nigga, you crazy.

Elegba

How much you want for looking at her, Size Number
One?

Ogun Size

Nothing, man.
It's cool.

Elegba

Eh, thanks, Ogun man, that's nice of you.

Oshoosi Size

Yeah, man.

Ogun Size

Yeah, well, enjoy your car, Legba.
Get somebody teach you how to drive it.

Don't see how you can with the
Law pressin you . . .

Elegba
It ain't mine.

Ogun Size
I thought you just said . . .

Elegba
I brought it here for Osi.

Ogun Size *and* **Oshoosi Size**
A car? A car.

Elegba
Yeah. Man.
Here.
Here.

Act Two

Oshoosi Size and Elegba follow the action described by Ogun.

Ogun Size
A week later . . .
Ogun Size is sleeping,
Dreaming.

Ogun Size

Ogun Size
And in his dream
Is his brother Oshoosi
And his friend Legba.

Oshoosi Size

Elegba

Ogun Size
In this dream of Ogun's
There is something strange
Happening.
His brother Oshoosi and Legba
Are bound together.
And they seem to want to part ways,
To separate.
But they can't.

Oshoosi Size

Elegba

Ogun Size
They can't seem to get loose of one another.

Oshoosi Size

Elegba

For a moment
In this dream of Ogun's
It seems that Elegba has changed
His heart.
And now stead of trying to get away from
Shoosi he staying with him,
Doing everything he can to be next to him.
And now Shoosi looking confused . . .

Oshoosi Size

Elegba

Ogun Size

Not knowing what to do,
Where to go, how to move,
Just feeling trapped,
Feeling caught up in Legba.
Wanting to get shed of Legba
But not knowing how.
Ogun wants to tell his brother
To call him . . .
'Call me, Shoosi, I will help you.'
But nothing comes out of his mouth
And nothing changes.
Ogun Size wants to fix this dream,
Right this wrong,
But it's too late.
Ogun's dream ends
And Elegba is dragging
His brother Oshoosi along with him
And there ain't nothing he can do about it!

Ogun Size
Ogun waking up.
OSI!

Oshoosi Size
Coming in.
What?

Ogun Size
Oshoosi?

Oshoosi Size
What you screaming for?

Ogun Size
Hey, man, listen . . .

Oshoosi Size
What's wrong, Og?
Man, you sweatin.

Ogun Size
Yeah, I was just . . .
Sleeping.

Oshoosi Size
You sleeping, that's some shit.

Ogun Size
It was a nap, you know . . .

Oshoosi Size
Naps for old folk, Ogun.
You getting old . . .

Ogun Size
Yeah, I guess.
I mean . . .

Oshoosi Size
I'm just messing with you, man.
Eh man, listen, thank you for the car, man.

Ogun Size
Well, see, that's . . .
The thing . . . I mean, I fixed it for you . . .

Oshoosi Size
I know, I know . . . I need a job. But I am looking
and I think the Food Lion is gone be my best bet.

Ogun Size
That's . . .

Oshoosi Size
Man, I damn sure don't want to . . .
But eh, wouldn't be called work if I wanted
To do it.

Ogun Size
Lil brother . . .

Oshoosi Size
But you got a career in the cars, man.
You love doin that?

Ogun Size
Yeah, I love fixing . . .

Oshoosi Size
I need to find something like that for myself.
That car look beautiful.
You seen it?
Course you seen it, you fixed it.

Ogun Size
Like? You can . . .

Oshoosi Size
I was thinking about going to school.

Ogun Size
Oh. Oh yeah?

Oshoosi Size
Yeah, man, take some classes take one of them
aptitude tests or something . . .
I took something like that in the pen . . .
You know, it said something like I should work in
social work.
I'm supposed to be sensitive to other people's needs
and shit . . .

Ogun Size
Nigga . . .

Oshoosi Size
Ha, I'm serious.
I just want to find something like you got . . .
But with lots of vacations time, man . . .
I want to see so much.
So much . . .
See everything.
In the pen I would sit in the library . . .

Ogun Size
Oshoosi . . .

Oshoosi Size
They had this one book was this big-ass book full of
pictures of Madagascar.
I mean just the people, the places, the water, the
eating, the ground, the earth, the fucking fecundity!

Ogun Size
Fe . . .
Fecundity?

Oshoosi Size
You like that!

Ogun Size
Ha, yeah!

Oshoosi Size
All these black-and-white and colour pictures,
    no words.
One of the reasons why I picked it up probably . . .
I'm a' start reading more!
I ain't no idiot, I mean I should read about this world . . .
I wanna go.

Ogun Size
Osi.

Oshoosi Size
I want to go to Madagascar!
Hell, I wanna go to Mexico, man, it's right there!
Right there and I ain't ever been.

Ogun Size
What?

Oshoosi Size
You know what fucked me up, Og?
This what got me, man . . .
I am looking at this book and I am thinking, 'Wow,
    this place look far away, far as hell . . .' This place
    out there, these people ain't even got on no clothes
    hardly and then I see it.

Ogun Size
What?

Oshoosi Size
This man . . .
This nigga . . .
This man . . .
He look just like me!
I swear somebody trying to fuck with me . . .

Legba or the Warden done got a picture of me and
    stuck it in this book about Madagascar with me
    half naked n' shit . . .
But it ain't!
Him and me could've been twins, man!
He standing and, you know, what he saying . . .
What it look like he saying?
'Come on, let's go.'
I can see it in his eyes!
I need to be out there looking for the me's.
He got something to tell me, man.
Something about me that I don't know, cause I am
    living here and all I see here are faces telling me
    what's wrong with me.
Maybe the me in China can tell me why I can't sleep
    at night.
Shit, man, who knows . . .
Man!
Ha. Ha.
I smoked too much today talking shit, right?

Ogun Size
Nah, man, you . . .
Wait, you smoked?

Oshoosi Size
Yeah, just a lil bit . . .

Ogun Size
Osi!

Oshoosi Size
Don't worry about it.
The Food Lion don't give drug tests, besides it's
    weed . . .
It ain't like I was shooting up or some dumb shit
    like that.

Ogun Size
I know . . .

Oshoosi Size
I'm doing good, Og, you don't got to worry about me.
Eh man, your work ain't being done in vain, man.
I love what you did to the ride, man.
That shit is . . . it's beautiful.
I love you for it.
I mean, when you brought it home today I was like,
damn it man, it look so I good I don't want to touch it.

Ogun Size
It's yours . . .

Oshoosi Size
I'm going be real careful in it.

Ogun Size
Please . . .

Oshoosi Size
Yeah, I know . . .
Me and Legba just going to the Outlet . . .
Gone see what's playing at the pictures.
Mostly going to see the women that come out for the
pictures.
I got enough for gas but not for the movie.
Hell, ain't nothing out really that I want to see.
Would like to see some thongs walk by.
And once they see me and Legba and that sparkling
ride they wanna show me they panny line.
I am down for inspection.

Elegba
From outside.
Beep!

Ogun Size
What the hell?

Oshoosi Size
That must be Legba out there fucking around.

Ogun Size
Eh man . . .

Oshoosi Size
Laughing. To Elegba:
Eh man!
Nigga!

Ogun Size
Osi . . .

Oshoosi Size
I got it, Og.

Elegba
Beep!

Oshoosi Size
Ha ha!
Eh nigga!
Stop wearing out my horn, I'm coming.
They arrest niggas just for that these days . . .
Get your arm out my window.

Ogun Size
Osi.

Oshoosi Size
Yeah, Og?

Elegba
Beep!

Oshoosi Size
Keep on, Krazy Kat.

Ogun Size
Eh.

Oshoosi Size
I'm a' be fine . . .
Fo sho.
Go back to sleep, Og.
Go head.
Oshoosi exits.

SCENE THREE

Elegba
Elegba standing in the early morning air, outside
At Oshoosi's window.
Oshoosi, calling . . .
Oshoosi Size.
You hear me . . .
I know you do . . .
If you in there I know you hear what Legba say.

Ogun Size
Ogun Size enters,
With his shovel . . .
He sees Elegba at his brother's window.
Deep breath.

Elegba
Hey . . . Size Number One,
How you doin?
You up early this morning . . .

Ogun Size
Morning, Legba . . .
Oshoosi still sleep, man,
You have to come back later on
If you wanna talk.

Elegba
So he here . . .

Ogun Size
You need something?

Elegba
You saw him? He here?

Ogun Size
Legba . . .

Elegba
I just want to tell him something.

Ogun Size
What, it can't wait till . . .

Elegba

Ogun Size

Elegba

Ogun Size
What you . . .
What's happening, Legba?

Elegba

Ogun Size
What's wrong?
Something wrong with my brother?
What's . . . You hear me talking to you, nigga?

Elegba
Why you up so early?

Ogun Size
I'm always up this early!

Elegba
You been working on that little piece of road
For a minute there.

Ogun Size
What you know about me?
That ain't no problem for you,
Is it?
What you come to tell my brother?

Elegba
Ask him.

Ogun Size
How he know if you ain't told him yet?

Elegba
He just ain't told you yet.

Ogun Size
So you got riddles for me this day,
Legba.

Elegba
You shouldn't be out here this early.
You should be sleeping or something . . .
It's still night it's so early.

Ogun Size
You got something to say to me, say it.

Elegba
I told you who I come for.

Ogun Size
Well, he in my house and I say he sleep.

Elegba
Keep him there . . . locked up in your spot
Size Number One
Cause if the law catch him . . .

Ogun Size

Elegba
Go in the house, Ogun.

It's too early for you to be out here.
You don't know who you run into this late at night,
This early in the morning.
Go in the house . . .

Ogun Size

I run into you, Legba.
I run into you.

Elegba

Go on building your way, Ogun.
Go on . . . we ain't need talk this morning.
You don't need to hear what Legba say.

Ogun Size

Don't do me no favours, Legba,
You hear me . . .
Don't hold nothing back that's
Gone beat me down later.
Go head and say what you gone say.

Elegba

How come you never like me, Size Number One?

Ogun Size

Legba, you trying to pull some bullshit?
Hear me. You trying something else?
Now you got something going on,
Let me find out what it is from you, man.
Cause I swear if I find out later and you
Could have told me when I see you,
I'm put my foot through you clean!

Elegba

Ogun Size

Elegba

One night we was in . . . we was locked up,
He hadn't been in there that long.
Hell, I hadn't been in long . . .

But he just got there
And he was strong.
Quiet to hisself.
Singing to hisself always
Most beautiful man ever seen.
He . . . call for you . . .
One night he just say, 'I want my brother,
Somebody call my brother . . .'
Crying it like a child scared of the boogie-monster
    coming,
This grown man, this man,
Crying for his brother . . .
Sobbing into the night,
'Og, come for Shoosi now . . .
Come on now.'
And at first I thought, 'Oh hell they gone get him for
    that.
They gone hurt him for being so soft,'
But nah, there was a wail in that call,
He call on you so hard,
Call for his brother like pastors call on Jesus,
Wanting for you like the sun wants to shine!
Can't do nothing but grieve for a man who miss his
    brother like that.
Sound like a bear trapped in some flesh-tearing snare
    hollering like that.
Can't mock no man in that much earthly pain.
He cry out and, hell, he make us all miss our brothers,
The ones we ain't neva even have.
All the jailhouse quiet,
The guards stop like a funeral coming down the halls
In respect, respect of this man mourning the loss of
    his brother,
And you just hear the clanging of that man voice
Bouncing on the cement and the steel . . . chiming like
    a bell

Till he calm down . . . till he just whispering your
   name now . . .
'My brother . . . my brother . . . where my brother . . .'
Gurgling it up out from under the tears . . .
'My brother . . .'

Ogun Size

Elegba

I look down at my feet, I say I got to meet him . . .
That brother . . . that brother that make a man get on
   his knees and cry out for
That brother! I say to myself I got to meet him . . .
I need to meet this brother,
Ogun Size.

Ogun Size

Sorry to disappoint you, Legba.

Elegba

Nah, nigga, you ain't disappoint Legba – you surprise
   me, but you ain't disappoint me. See, I ain't had no
   hope in you, I ain't the one you disappoint when
   you don't come visit and you don't write more than
   few words for letters. No, you ain't disappoint me,
   nah. I ain't the one.

Ogun Size

Elegba

I can't never be his brother like you his brother.
Never.
You know that right.
No need to hate Legba.
I can't stop you from being his brother.

Ogun Size

Elegba

The law might come round this morning.
He might come round here looking for a Size.

I ain't saying which one.
Not sure if he know which Size he want.
But seeing as how he ain't got you . . .
Must be another Size he want try on.
Must be another Size he ain't catch up with yet.
Always a way to go.
Gone head to work, Ogun.
Gone to your shop.

Ogun Size

Elegba
Go on.

Ogun Size
Ogun exits to work.

SCENE FOUR

Ogun Size
Slam.
Since day one . . .
Day one,
You been fucking up . . .
Not just the other day when you was standing here,
Looking all lost and stupid, all high on life,
And the little bit of weed that Food Lion won't find
    in your piss.
Nah, hell nah.
FROM DAY ONE.
Aunt Elegua stopped taking us to church.
I stopped going cause I ain't want to go in the first
    place.
But you kept getting up in the morning, you kept
    getting up every Sabbath,
And going down to the river to wash your fucking sins
    away . . .

And everybody say, 'Look at Little Size taking up the
    cross with Jesus.'
'Look at him, he only nine.'
'Look at that devotion for Jesus!'
'You should do like your brother, Ogun . . . You
    should go to church like Shoosi!'
You know what I wanted to say? 'Fuck that, nigga,
    and the church.'
I was jealous.
I was.
I have to admit that right here in your face, I say,
    'Why couldn't I be devoted like Oshoosi?'
Why didn't I want to sit in the boring-ass church all
    day and listen to the hypocrites sing songs on high
    to a God that ain't listening? Cause he wasn't, he
    ain't, he wasn't then and he ain't now . . . I been
    praying for yo ass like a fool and no God! No God,
    just sun and work and fuck-ups from you . . .
I wanted to be you for a moment, Little Size, I wanted
    to be just like my little brother until me and Elegua
    found you using the money you was stealing from
    collection in a crap game.
Yeah. Yeah.
And then everything turned.
Everything turned. Spun right round. Landed on me.
Everybody like, 'He only nine.'
'If you would have been a better role model for him,
    Ogun, he wouldn't acted like this,'
If I would've . . . If I . . .
But Aunt Elegua sealed it, though . . . that miserable
    old ass lady . . .
She made my whole world crash down in front of
    me . . . She say, 'Your mama would have been so
    disappointed in you . . . Letting your brother go like
    that. Yemoja would have hated you failing her,
    Ogun. Letting your brother go.' Letting you go . . .

I let you go? I let you go. Me. She said Mama
name . . . she never say Mama name but she threw
that shit in my face.
I got one image of my mama in my mind, one . . . and
it fucks with me at night . . . You hear me, it's the
shit that keep me up building a fucking driveway
to no
Where . . .
Shit that won't let you lay down right . . .
She standing near the water, my mama standing out
looking out, looking out towards the gulf, belly full
of you and she standing there holding my hand.
Tight.
Tight.
Tight.
Just her and the water . . .
Us. That's all I got left of my mama, and you in that
picture. You a part of all I got left, nigga.
So when Aunt Elegua in all her wisdom decided to
make my ass feel guilty about you, that thought,
that thought . . . spring up in my head . . . my
mama holding my brother inside and me tight,
gripping.
So I held on from that day . . .
I gripped onto your ass and pushed you through
school . . . I forced you up and out . . .
Whatever the fuck you . . . I did it . . . I burned my
chance at anything so that I didn't leave you behind
. . . I would run after you and ahead of you, always
hoping that I could keep my grip on you or at least
catch you before anyone else did.
But no matter what I did . . . No matter if I thought
you were fine . . . I thought you were gonna be
okay, somehow you would slip through and fuck
up and fuck up and fuck up and when you fucked
up somehow I fucked up! Somehow there is no

escaping you! You say I ain't never been in the pen?
Nigga, whenever you fall everyone look at me like
I fucking pushed you . . . That's my fucking life
sentence . . . That's my lockdown . . . All my life
I carry your sins on my back . . . And now you out
there riding around in a car that I souped up and
popped off only so they could find you in it with a
fucking pound of powder! YEYO!
What the fuck?

Oshoosi Size

It wasn't mine, Ogun . . .

Ogun Size

Shut up! Shut up, shut the fuck up. You shut up don't
say a fucking . . . You fucked up . . . Say that! You
wanna say something, for once in your life say
something for me . . . You fucked up, you fucked
up, you fucked up, you fucked up you fucked up
you fucked up, you fucked up you fucked up you
fucked up you fucked up you fucked up you fucked
up you fucked up you fucked up you fucked up.
You fucked up!

Oshoosi Size

I.

Ogun Size

You fucked up.

Oshoosi Size

He . . .

Ogun Size

You fucked up.

Oshoosi Size

I fucked up.

Ogun Size

Oshoosi Size

Ogun Size
So what you doin in here, hiding out?

Oshoosi Size
I don't need that shit from you . . .
You don't know what you talking about.
I ain't did nothing.

Ogun Size
That ain't what Legba say.
Hell, that ain't what the law say.
The law, that's right.
He come to my door at the shop today and
Say he looking for the other Size.
I say, 'What you talking about?'
Say he looking for the other Size . . .
I say ain't but one Size here.
My heart sink down, Shoosi . . .
My heart drop down, I swear to God it did.
You was doing so good. So good.
Even when Legba say that you might be in trouble
I ain't believe. Wasn't till the law come up on me like
    that.

Oshoosi Size
I ain't did nothing!

Ogun Size
What, he lying?
Say he lying, Shoosi.
Please, tell me how he . . .
If you convince me he lying I'm with you . . .
Tell me how he lying, Oshoosi!
The law running around here . . .
Looking for you . . .
I . . . don't wanna know . . .
Yeah, I do . . .

But . . . I . . .
You gotta . . .
You have to . . .
Please . . .
You have to . . . C'mon . . .

Oshoosi Size

Legba and me was going to the outlet. He had a gym
bag out there, said he had to spend the night near
the bayou.

Said his cousin Nia was gone let him stay with her
for a while out by the water.

I didn't know what the hell was in the bag. How the
hell I know what he carrying? Man say he spending
the night at his cousin.

I think he got clothes in the muthafucker.

The night was going good, Ogun, you know . . .

It was right . . .

We left the pictures, we look at the girls for a minute,
few of 'em smiling . . . few of 'em laughing. But you
know he want me to drive out there, wanted me to
go out there . . . And drop him off.

So I say okay.

What laws I break?

Huh . . . Tell me . . .

I drove too fast out to Nia's. Yeah, that I did do, cause
I remembered how phyne she use to be . . . I wanted
to see if I could get at her . . . See if I could lay there
for a while . . . Blocka. Get that pussy. I had sin on
my mind but not in my heart. So I was racing. And
I'm just going and I got the wind coming in the car
and the songs playing and Legba laughing, cause
we having a good time . . . It's nice out . . . ain't too
hot yet . . . And . . . and I'm driving and singing . . .
(*Sings a song.*) Just feel right that they played it.
Like Nia singing it to me, you know. Inviting me
to spend the night too. I'm singing and I caught

a breeze right in my nose, that brackish water breeze
right in my fucking nose and I sneezed . . . and the
car spun right round. And I stopped and snot was
hanging out my nose, I was laughing my ass off,
it was so funny. Legba was laughing and it was
dark and shit . . . It was real dark and laughing and
then . . . And then . . .
Felt like a fucking dream. Music still playing,

Elegba enters singing.

Ogun stand watching.

Oshoosi Size
I felt like I had been there before.

Elegba
(*sings*)

Oshoosi Size
Just us out there . . . Just the car sitting and chillin
hearing that ole music . . . hearing it say something
but really just telling me that I'm free and everything
alright . . . Legba say, Legba say –

Elegba
This nice, man.

Oshoosi Size
I say, 'Yeah man.
Yeah, it is.'
He say, 'Let's . . .'

Elegba
Let's just sit for a minute . . .

Oshoosi Size
I say, 'Alright, man,
But no too long, gotta get to your cousin.'

Elegba
Yeah, but this nice, right?

Oshoosi Size

He say, 'This nice . . .'

I say, 'Yeah man, you right.' It was, Ogun. I ain't gone
lie. I never felt like that. Just sitting and being cool.
I mean, I just forgot life could be good sitting still.
You try to tell me to be still but I ain't listen. Not
till I near bout run off the side of the road I realise
life can be sweet still. I smell that gulf air. Just
making me think more of Nia. Remember her body.
How she walk like. Music making me sleepy.

Elegba

(*sings*)

Oshoosi Size

Making me sleepy and hard at the same time . . .
Why that happen Ogun, why when you get sleepy
yo dick hard? Guess that mystery to be solved by
scientists and astrologers or people who got plenty
of time to study dick . . . All this a dream, it was so
quiet out there . . .

Elegba

(*sings*)

Elegba *and* **Oshoosi Size**

(*hum*)

Oshoosi Size

(*sings*)

Elegba

Elegba touches Oshoosi head.

Oshoosi Size

It couldn't been happening.

Elegba

Let's, let's stay for a second.
Legba's hand rests on Shoosi shoulder.

Oshoosi Size
Not for real . . .

Elegba
(*hums*)
His hand slides down . . .

Oshoosi Size
Not like that.

Elegba
(*sings*)
Slides down onto his thigh.

Oshoosi Size
And then I heard sirens.
Come out nowhere, lights and sirens.
Music playing.
The Law come up on us looking like he happy bout
    something.
Shining his light.
'You got anything in the trunk, son?'
'No, sir.'
Nothing was in there as far as I know.
Legba should've spoke the fuck up.
If he knew something was back there shoulda said
    something.
'No, sir.'
'Well, what in the shit is this?'
I hate how some niggas don't know how to cuss right.
Who say what in the shit?
'What in the shit is this?'
Huh . . . uh uh uh.
He standing holding this bag wide open.
He ain't supposed to search the car unless he got
    provocation
So he know he wrong but dammit if the sheriff ain't
    standing there holding Legba's bag
And it's pouring white out onto the asphalt.

I be damned.
I wish you could've seen my face . . .
I wish you could've,
Hell I wish I coulda.
I like to jump over and kill Legba
But the law say get out the car.
I say, 'Legba, what the fuck he holding, man?
What you doing?'
He just looking.
Almost like he smiling.
I say, 'Tell him that shit ain't mine, man.'
He ain't say nothing.
Just stand there.
I say, 'Say that shit ain't mine, Legba.'
He ain't say shit.
The law walk back over to his car smiling his big-ass
    smile.
That 'I got you' smile.
That cat-caught-mouse smile.
Beaming from around his fat-ass head . . . Beaming.
I look at Legba and he still ain't saying shit . . .
He ain't doing shit.
And I see where he at already . . . I see where Legba at.
He in jail.
That's where . . .
He gone. He already sitting in his cell singing.

Elegba
(*sings*)

Oshoosi Size
He back there just that fast.

Elegba
(*sings*)

Oshoosi Size
And I see him go there . . .
I see them walls around him . . .

Elegba

(*sings*)

Oshoosi Size

I see them dark-ass halls and the midnights with no
sleep.

I swear I see 'em, Ogun, as you my brother I see 'em.

Elegba

(*sings*)

Oshoosi Size

And I can't.

I just can't.

So I ran.

I can't tell you what I ran like, how I ran . . . what
I saw when I ran . . .

I ran . . .

I run all the way till I get here.

And I come in here and I close the door and I say
I ain't going back . . .

I ain't going back.

Ogun Size

Ogun Size stares at his brother.

Oshoosi Size

Oshoosi Size his younger brother.

Oshoosi Size

I am here now . . . Brother Size . . .

I'm here. What we gone do?

Ogun Size
That same night.

Oshoosi Size
Later on.

Ogun Size
Laughing . . .

Oshoosi Size
. . . His ass off,
I swear to God.

Ogun Size
Nigga, you lying!

Oshoosi Size
You trying to tell me you ain't say it?

Ogun Size
I ain't neva said no shit like . . .

Oshoosi Size
I remember it . . .
I remember it like it was yesterday.
Roon had just came round the house and told us that
    Mama finally passed,
Finally came over to the house . . .
I was little but I wasn't that damn little.
Roon came over there and told Aunt Elegua, 'She
    gone, Ele.'
That's how he say it . . . He say, 'She gone, Ele. Yemoja
    finally let go.'
I never did know what that meant, 'finally' . . .
I mean. I know now . . .
Anyway Roon turn around and see us standing there
    and walk over to us.

And he said, 'Lil men, yo mama ain't coming here to
   get you.
She went to be a part of the number.
She went on with the father now.
Y'all don't be sad or scared.
Yo mama ain't coming.'
He say, 'You understand, lil man?'
Getting all close in my face breath smelling like
   snuff . . .
All loud.
'YOU UNDERSTAND, LIL MAN?'
I say, 'Yeah I hear you.'
Anything to get yo ass out my face.
'I gotcha.'
He look at you, he say, 'You be strong, Ogun,'
And I swear you could see the tremor start in your
   face . . .

Ogun Size
   Hahah!
   Shut up . . .

Oshoosi Size
   Like the Mississippi swelling up.
   You so ugly when you cry.
   If you cried today I still bet it's ugly . . .
   You say . . .

Ogun Size
   Go on now.

Oshoosi Size
   You say,
   'LORD GOD . . . WILL THIS PAIN . . . EVER GO
   AWAY?!'
   Knees buckled from under you.
   Falling on the ground grabbing up the carpet
   underneath you.

Convulsing and weeping and wailing like Mary.
I like to cried cause I thought you was gonna die.
I say, 'Lord, you done took my mama, not my brother
too.'

Ogun Size

Hahah!
It ain't funny, Oshoosi.
I was in grief.

Oshoosi Size

You ass was overdramatic!

Ogun Size

Hah!

Oshoosi Size

Then Aunt Ele kept calling you carpet boy for so long
after.

Ogun Size

That woman don't got a sympathetic bone in her body.

Oshoosi Size

But damn sure got a lotta body.

Ogun Size

You ain't neva lied.

Oshoosi Size

Then gone have the nervc to have a fainting spell at
Mama's funeral.
Fat ass . . .

Ogun Size

Like somebody could hold her big ass up.

Oshoosi Size

Thank God for O Li Roon,
Because I wasn't about to try and revive her nothing.
Her big ass passed out,

I say, let her stay out, that teach her ass for fainting.
I wasn't going nowhere near her.

Ogun Size
Hateful Aunt Elegua.

Oshoosi Size
Sitting over there old as she wanna be.
Like she ain't never gone die.
Walking negro spirtual.
Just keep rolling along.

Ogun Size
Seem like she never liked us,
Like she resented Mama for getting sick
And having to take us in.

Oshoosi Size
Wasn't like we didn't come with two nice welfare
    cheques
To go long with us.
Hell, the government might as well put money clips
    round us and handed us to her.

Ogun Size
And she still jipped us at Christmas.

Oshoosi Size
Ain't that some shit?
Thank God for Santa Claus.

Ogun Size
You believe in Santa?

Oshoosi Size
My big brother leaving me presents under the tree . . .
Yeah, I believe.

Ogun Size
You knew it was me?

Oshoosi Size
> Who else it gone be?
> Nobody else care.

Ogun Size

Oshoosi Size
> You act like you don't care . . .
> You act like you so tough, but I would catch it . . .
> I catch you looking at me sometimes like you wanna
>   beat my ass you so mad.
> Then I see this smile crack.
> I see it and I see you . . .

Ogun Size

Oshoosi Size

Ogun Size
> What you do in prison?

Oshoosi Size
> Man, why you always ask that?

Ogun Size
> You know what I do when you was gone . . .

Oshoosi Size

Ogun Size
> Think about what you was doing right then.
> Try to see if I could think what you was doing in the
>   pen.
> Sometimes a bad spell would hit me and my mind see
>   terrible things happening to you. Fights, and wonder
>   how you sleeping.
> Sometimes I see you in there smiling big.
> That's one thing about you I do know . . .
> You kind to everybody.
> You give everybody a chance and, yeah, you fuck up
>   but that's how the world balance you out.

All that niceness you pass to everybody they take it
and it comes back so that when you do fuck up you
paying for it ain't so bad.
You good to everybody you meet.
I thought you come out of the pen hardcore, dark and
mad as hell.
You came out same cool-ass Oshoosi, laid back
laughing smiling thinking about pussy. Only thing
prison made you was tired.

Oshoosi Size
You right, Og, I'm tired, man. So tired.
Tired. Too tired to fight it off.

Ogun Size
Ogun staring at his brother not knowing what to say.

Oshoosi Size
Oshoosi looking at the ground thinking of all he done
said . . .

Ogun Size
Nothing more to say . . .

Oshoosi Size
Weary of saying anything.

Ogun Size
Weary of talking.

Oshoosi Size *and* **Ogun Size**
Weary

Ogun Size
(*sings a little, badly*)

Oshoosi Size
Aw hell, nah.
I'm already on the cusp of crazy – you trying to push
me over?

Ogun Size
What?

Oshoosi Size
Nigga, you know you can't sing.

Ogun Size
Eh, the song just popped into my head.

Oshoosi Size
Pop it out.

Ogun Size
Eh, I use to sing you to sleep.

Oshoosi Size
No. I use to close my ears until I passed out.

Ogun Size
Ha.
You the singer.

Oshoosi Size
Nah man, you crazy.

Ogun Size
Sing that song for me. I want to hear it.

Oshoosi Size
Nah, c'mon, Og.

Ogun Size
You ain't sleeping no time soon.
Me neither.
Morning ain't for a while yet – sing something, man.
I ain't heard you in a long time.
Not full out.
I mean, I hear you in the shower.
But c'mon, sing for me.

Oshoosi Size

Ogun Size

Oshoosi Size
I tell you what . . .

Ogun Size
What?

Oshoosi Size
Play back-up for me.

Ogun Size
What!

Oshoosi Size
Don't act like you ain't never done it before.

Ogun Size
Nigga . . .

Oshoosi Size
Hold on . . .

Ogun Size
Where you going?

Oshoosi Size
Hold the hell on.
Coming.
I'll be right there.
Turns on music.
(*Says the title and artist of song.*)

Ogun Size
That sweet song start playing.
I didn't know you had this song.

Oshoosi Size
Every man need a copy of this song.

Ogun Size
Man, you use to sing the hell out of this song.

Oshoosi Size
Still do.
But I need a piano, man.

Ogun Size
You mean an organ, man.

Oshoosi Size
Ah nigga, just play whatever, but in the back.

Ogun Size
Alright, Ike, I'm getting.

Oshoosi Size
Singing with the music . . .

Ogun Size
I think I'm a switch to drums.

Oshoosi Size
Good work, brother.

Ogun Size
I thought you would enjoy that, brother.
C'mon, sing the song.

Oshoosi Size
(*sings*)

Ogun Size
Yeah!

Oshoosi Size
(*sings*)

Ogun Size
What you got do?

Oshoosi Size
(*sings*)

Ogun Size *and* **Oshoosi Size**
(*sing at the same time*)

Oshoosi Size
Laughing.
Eh, you kinda overstepping your boundaries, piano-sax
man.

Ogun Size
Having a good time . . .
Eh man, I am just backing you up.
Just sing the song, Anna Mae.

Oshoosi Size
(*sings*)

Ogun Size
Now you getting into it!
But don't turn into a Temptation.
Keep it cool.

Oshoosi Size
Let me do this!

Ogun Size
You got it.

Oshoosi Size
(*sings*)

Ogun Size
Playing back up and
Doing Temptation moves.

Oshoosi Size
(*sings*)
Laughing!

Ogun Size
Cracking up!

Oshoosi Size
(*sings*)

Ogun Size
Smiling.

Oshoosi Size
(*sings*)

Elegba
Elegba appears at the window,
Like a glimmer of moonlight
For a moment, is gone.

Oshoosi Size
Oshoosi sees it,
How could he not?
He stops singing.

Ogun Size
What happened?

Oshoosi Size
Tired.
Voice tired.

Ogun Size
C'mon, man, finish.

Oshoosi Size
I can't, man.

Ogun Size
Eh, brother, just try to . . .

Oshoosi Size
Eh, man I'm done . . .

Ogun Size
But Oshoo, you . . .
C'mon, man, you the star.
Shine, little brother . . .

Oshoosi Size
I don't want to play no more.

Ogun Size
    Brother . . .

Oshoosi Size
    Eh, stop pushing me, Og.
    I said I am done, man.
    I'm going to bed.

Ogun Size

Oshoosi Size
    Oshoosi Size exits to bed.

Ogun Size
    Ogun Size is left alone.
    Without his brother.
    The music plays in the background.

Ogun Size
    The music turns off.
    Just the sound of night, now.

Ogun Size
    Okay man.
    Okay.
    Good night.

Ogun Size
    Ogun Size
    Stands alone in the night.
    Staring.

Ogun Size

Ogun Size

Ogun Size

Ogun Size

Ogun Size

Ogun Size

Ogun Size
And the next morning

SCENE SIX

Ogun Size
Ogun Size enters.
Osi!

Ogun Size
Calling for his brother,
Osi . . .
Oshoosi Size!

Oshoosi Size
Waking up, coming in.
Og, man,
Why you calling?

Ogun Size
Get up.

Oshoosi Size
What time is it?

Ogun Size
Time to go.

Oshoosi Size
Eh man, look . . .

Ogun Size
Get up!

Oshoosi Size
The court house open today till five .

Ogun Size
You gotta go.

Oshoosi Size
It ain't even five in the morning yet.

Ogun Size
I said get it up!

Oshoosi Size
What you talking about, man?
What you doin?

Ogun Size
THROW.

Oshoosi Size
Eh man, that's all my shit!

Ogun Size
Get it together . . .

Oshoosi Size
Why you . . .
Ogun, why you doing this, brother?

Ogun Size
Let's go!

Oshoosi Size
Brother . . . Brother Size, man . . .

Ogun Size
You got to get outta here.

Oshoosi Size
You just . . .
You upset!
What you mad at?
What, you don't believe me?
Og!

Ogun!
Man . . . don't do me like this!

Ogun Size
Get your shit.
Get in the truck.

Oshoosi Size
Og.

Ogun Size
Don't come back.
Don't call me, hear?
Don't write . . .
When they come here . . .
When the law comes here for you . . .
I'm going to deny you . . .
They gone ask for my brother . . .
I'm going to say I ain't got none . . .
He gone say, 'There two Size.'
I'm gone say, 'Nah, just one. Only one . . .'
I'm a deny you . . .
Up to three times . . .
That's all I can take. That's how many times I can
   do it . . .
Don't cry when you hear about it . . .
Don't think I don't know you . . .
Don't believe it . . . Hear me . . .
You here with me . . .
Always . . .
But you gotta go fore you get caught . . .
Get in the truck, all your shit, brother . . .
Everything you need . . .
Need, Shoosi, need . . .
Only stop when you need . . .
So don't stop till you free . . .
Don't stop . . .
Open your hand.

Oshoosi Size
What!

Ogun Size
Open your hand!

Oshoosi Size
Okay . . .

Ogun Size
This it . . .
This everything . . .
All I got, it's yours.
Here, Oshoosi.

Oshoosi Size
Og man, don't do this . . .

Ogun Size
It's done . . .
Get in the truck . . .
Take it . . .
Go south . . .
See Mexico.

Oshoosi Size
Mexico . . .

Ogun Size
It's right there and you ain't never been . . . right?

Oshoosi Size

Ogun Size
What you waiting on, man?

Oshoosi Size

Ogun Size
Man, don't let them put you back in there.
I wanna know you still my brother somewhere . . .
Anywhere in the world.

You still my brother . . .
I swear.
Out there you will still be a Size, Oshoosi Size,
Brother to Ogun.

Oshoosi Size

Ogun Size
I fixed the truck for you.
If it act up on you,
If it start bucking, don't stop,
Hit it and call my name.
The truck know me . . .
It'll carry you on . . .

Oshoosi Size
Oshoosi Size, breaking down . . .

Ogun Size
Ogun, trying to hold it.
It's alright . . .
It's alright, brother.
It's gone be alright.
I believe you.
I do.
Just go.
Go find you.
When you meet him,
Ask him if he remember me.
Ask him.
Ask.

Oshoosi Size

Ogun Size

Oshoosi Size

Ogun Size

Oshoosi Size

Oshoosi Size leaves his brother Ogun Size
Standing in the early morning . . .

Ogun Size

Ogun Size sees it, how can he not, and is left alone in
the early foreday in the morning mist.

End of play.